The Simplicity of Spirituality

The Simplicity of Spirituality

YOUR GUIDE TO THE 5TH DIMENSION

Beverly Scott

To order additional copies of this book, contact:
Xlibris Corporation
1-888-795-4274
www.Xlibris.com
Orders@Xlibris.com
76442

Contents

"The only way our planet is going to make it through these difficult times is by bringing more compassion to it."

—Dr. James Martin Peebles

Acknowledgements

This book would not have been possible without the great care and consideration on behalf of my friend Audrae Gardner, and the guidance of the spirits Dr. James Martin Peebles, Gabriel and John. Were it not for Dr. Peebles himself, this book would not have been written at all.

To learn more about Dr. Peebles and his work visit *www.summerbacon.com*. Summer Bacon is a Trance Medium who has been working with, and channeling, Dr. Peebles for more than ten years. She is the clearest and truest channel I have come across, and I have experienced many.

Preface

The purpose of this book is to alleviate any fear you may have about your journey into the 5th Dimension; help you to understand just what the 5th dimension is, and to help you understand the turmoil going on in your life today, why your life and the world around you seems topsy turvy, and offer ways to make the transition into the 5th Dimension a little less mysterious, and a little more fun.

We will discuss your journey to the 5th Dimension, what you may encounter along the way, how to prepare yourself for the journey, and what is waiting for you there. I hope that as you read you find excitement, anticipation and joy at the perspective of what you are creating for yourself in your life, as you open yourself up to more of the spirit that you are, as your vibrational frequency increases to a higher and finer degree during your journey.

There is absolutely nothing to fear about the 5th Dimension or your journey there. It is not a physical destination, but a journey taking you deeper within yourself as you move closer and closer to the 5th dimension, where you will have more understanding of your Oneness with all that is. It is simply a different place to grow into greater communication with God, and the journey there is a wonderful adventure. You will not lose your personality in this process or when you arrive. You will be very much awake in your own consciousness. You will become more and more clear within self, and will be able to interact with others without all the mishmash of 3rd dimensional chaos.

You will better understand just who you are, how important you are to the world and to the Universe, and you will have a much deeper understanding of how things work in our world and in our Universe.

Introduction

This all started when Dr. James Martin Peebles, a spirit abiding in the 16th Dimension, told me that I was to write a book titled "The Finer Points of Energy." He said that it was to be about the 5th Dimension and our journey there should we decide to join our Planet Earth on her journey into the 5th Dimension.

"But I don't know anything about the 5th Dimension," I protested.

His response, "Look at your life and write the book."

Shortly after I received the information that I would be writing this book, and during an Open Session led by Summer Bacon, Dr. Peebles responded to a question from one of the attendees with, "So guess what? Everything that you have done, everything that you have said, every experience you have had, everything that you have felt, every word that you have spoken adds up to this moment here. This is what you created." This response of Dr. Peebles started me thinking, and I started looking back in retrospect at my life to see what had led me to this moment: this moment of writing a book having to do with the 5th dimension.

So with that said, here is a quick life review, hopefully taking the place of the life review we've heard we experience when we make our transition. Maybe this will do instead. Anyway, here we go . . .

Let's see now . . . I started questioning things in the Bible and wondering about God before I started Kindergarten, trying to find what to me were satisfactory answers to questions I had about what I was being taught in the established organized church. It just didn't make sense to me that I was being taught to fear God when the very first Bible verse I was told to memorize by my Sunday School teacher was, "God is love" part of 1st John 4:8, the full verse being "He who does not love does not know God;

for God is love." (A bit much for a four year old, so the "God is love" part worked for me.)

As I got older, and my search for truth continued, not only was I looking for some kind of confirmation of what I thought the teachings of Jesus Christ meant, I also wanted to know, and was asking the questions, "Where did I come from?," "Why am I here?" and "Where am I going?"

Only upon meeting Summer Bacon, and Dr. James Martin Peebles, the beautiful spirit and teacher whom Summer channels, were my questions answered in a way that made sense to me, that to me said exactly what Jesus Christ teaches in the New Testament of the Bible. And my questions, "Where did I come from?," "Why am I here?" and "Where am I going?" were answered as well.

I met Summer and Dr. Peebles as a result of being caught in an economic downturn of things in California, neither my husband nor I able to get a job after 40 years in the work force, so pack up we did, and moved to Arizona. After three business flops in Arizona and a 5 year law suit with a company we are still not allowed to mention, we found ourselves starting over at age 60. All of this occurred over a period of about eight years, spending one of those years homeless; not totally homeless just without a home of our own for the first time in forty years. So with all of our worldly goods in storage, and the most marvelous family anyone could ever wish for, I, by choice, lived from relative to relative, and my husband lived in a small 5th Wheel on the property of one of our daughters, close to where we had been living so that he could look for a job. He was welcome to live in her home of course, but he is a stubborn and very proud man, so chose to live in the 5th wheel instead.

While all of this was happening I prayed and prayed and prayed, and things just seemed to get worse. I didn't understand what was going on or why. I do now. Through all of this I never doubted God for a minute, and found that God really did know my needs before I did. [Ref Matthew 6:8]

A lot of tears were shed, a lot of "why me's" said during those years, and at least three times that I can remember there were moments of just wanting to throw in the towel, drive our car off a cliff and forget the whole thing, but . . . I knew that wasn't allowed, that I would just have to come back and do it all again, only the next time the lessons would be tougher. And since I had come this far, any decision other than to stick around and finish things up this trip would not be very bright on my part.

They were interesting years—certainly none that I would care to live again—but I wouldn't want to have missed them either. There's an enormous amount of growth to be had during these types of experiences.

What is really interesting about all of this is that when all was said and done, when it was all over, God saw to it that we had just enough, and I mean exactly enough financially to provide us with a roof over our heads, our very own roof, and the rest is history. We are happier than we have ever been, and having the time of our lives.

Not a pretty picture, but finally the wop along side the head by—not a 2X4, more like a 6X8—took hold in all of this, and things started looking up, and here I am writing a book about the 5th dimension. Talk about "expecting the unexpected," this is probably the most unexpected thing that has ever happened to me. There were a lot of difficult lessons along the way, but never losing faith and always trusting (and, I quote here, changing the "you" to "I"): "So guess what, everything that I have done, everything that I have said, every experience I have had, everything that I have felt, every word that I have spoken adds up to this moment here. This is what I created." Not bad for one lifetime, although Dr. Peebles told me this has taken several lifetimes to create, as I'm sure is the case for many of us. What I'm saying here is that as difficult as those years were, and as many times as I wanted to just throw in the towel, I didn't. And, I am so glad because if I had I wouldn't be experiencing the beautiful life I have now. There are still little bumps in the road, but guess what? It's all part of the journey, and life is so much richer because of those bumps.

So that's just a little bit of the story of how this all came about. I hope you enjoy the book and your journey into the 5th Dimension. It's a hoot! Remember, that which doesn't kill you makes you stronger. Enjoy the trip.

Chapter 1

WHAT IS THE 5TH DIMENSION?

The 5th dimension is a state of joy.

We are told by Jesus Christ in the New Testament of the Bible; John 14:2 "In my Father's house are many mansions: if it were not so I would have told you. I go to prepare a place for you."

Jesus is referring to the different dimensions that exist throughout our Universe and beyond, different areas of learning, none being any better or more important than the other, just as higher learning at the University level is no more important than Kindergarten in our learning process here in the 3rd dimension. Our Planet Earth has, up to this point, been abiding in what is known as the 3rd dimension, as have the majority of the human beings living here on our planet. We are here on this school called Plant Earth visiting the 3rd dimension to experience whatever it is we need to experience in order for us to grow and to expand into greater and greater love, growing closer and closer to God, as the illusion of our separation from God diminishes.

The 3rd dimension is where some of the heavier frequencies exist, heavier energies such as greed, anger, jealousy, war, hatred, the need to control, disease, and discomfort just to name a few; the basis of all of these 3rd dimensional frequencies being fear. Each one of these carry their own frequency band, and when we experience these feelings within us, then we are existing in that particular band or frequency; here again, not a place, but a frequency band, an energy that we have brought into our existence with our anger, our need to control, any word, thought or deed that we have chosen to participate in that is less than love. At any given moment we can exist in the 3rd dimension of fear, or the 5th dimension of joy and love. It's always our choice.

Not all human beings will choose to move into the 5th dimension, so think of the 5th dimension in terms of a movement on the earth, not the entire planet going there. We have a chance to move there, to change our minds about a lot of things, i.e., about hating someone and turning it into love. That's what the 5th dimension is: changing our minds, deciding to grow, and to move into the 5th dimension. Those who choose not to make the journey will either leave us, choosing to make their transition, or will stay where they are on their path and continue to abide in the 3rd dimensional frequency band of fear.

The 5th Dimension is simply the ongoing of our journey back to God with the refinement of our own frequencies as we grow. We are in a time period now where our Planet Earth is moving into the 5th Dimension. Consequently her frequencies are changing, and the things of the 3rd dimension are dissipating. As a result, our world as we know it is changing, our financial institutions are upside down, and our governments are in turmoil. At the same time we human beings are being given challenges to deal with and to learn from or not, depending on whether or not we have chosen to make the journey with our Planet Earth into the 5th Dimension. What we consider to be a recession, a depression or even the end of the world is actually the clearing out, the dissipation of, the cleaning up of the other side of the coin: one side of the coin being love, the other side, fear. We are all in this process together, moving out of fear, and we all have fear of one kind or another, and moving into love, realizing the love that we are and the love we want to give and to receive from the world.

Things that work for us here in the 3rd Dimension will not work for us in the 5th. Anger, fear, greed, dishonesty, our need to control, war, hatred, envy, coveting material things, these are all things of the 3rd Dimension existing at very slow and heavy vibrational frequencies. Consequently if we want to move along on our path into the 5th Dimension it is necessary that we release these lower frequencies from our existence, and that is what all the upheaval going on in our lives and on our Planet Earth is about right now. We are being given circumstances in our lives to look at and to study, opportunities to learn what is really important in our lives, and in that process to finally realize that the only security that exists is love for, and trust in, God. God is the constant, the only real thing we have going for us, the only thing we can depend on, the only thing that will never fail us.

The God that I am talking about here is, as stated in the Bible in the book of 1st John 1:5 God is light, 4:8 God is love; and again 4:16 God is love. If you prefer, you can call it a higher power, that which holds everything together, truth, Oneness, it doesn't matter what you call it, it's all the same thing. As we work our way into the 5th dimension we grow closer to the God that we are, as we choose to change our minds, as we choose to step out of the negative band of fear, and onto the path of more love.

Even now you may be experiencing the 5th dimension at times. There are so many dimensions, and we move from one to another all the time. We're not aware of it, but we do. For instance, when you are sitting in front of your computer, not doing anything in particular, just staring into space with nothing really going on, you are in the 1st, maybe the 2nd dimension, a place of birth where the potential of more exists. So you sit there just mulling things over, and suddenly something pops into your mind, you have birthed an idea, and there you are bringing your idea to fruition in the 3rd dimension.

TIME DOES NOT EXIST IN THE 5TH DIMENSION

The 5th dimension is a state of being, a state of living in the moment without fear, a state of being fully present in every moment. Again, the 5th Dimension is simply another area in which to grow into greater communication with God.

The 5th dimension is an area where time does not exist, and when time does not exist, pressure disappears. The need to be someplace at a given time, the need to learn something at a certain time is gone, all the pressure that time puts on us here in the 3rd dimension is gone. In the 5th dimension we are living in the moment, we are in the "now" enjoying the "now" to the fullest.

It's really interesting: when I was studying this part of my experience of the 5th dimension, my watch disappeared. I knew where and when I had worn it last. I remembered picking it up to put it away, and that's the last I remembered. I had no idea where it was, but I knew it was in the house someplace, and then one day when our daughters were visiting us from out of state one of them picked up an empty grocery bag that I keep in my room for recycling as a trash bag and—yup, you guessed it—she put her hand inside the bag and pulled out my watch. What a trip that was!

Two things happened for me during this experience. The first thing was that I didn't panic when I couldn't find my watch. I have misplaced and/or lost this particular watch four times in the past. I've had this watch for about 35 years and I love it. It's just a plain gold watch with a twisted gold chain as the band, but I love it, and whenever it was lost or misplaced in the past I panicked, I mean really, really panicked. Not this time. Not at all. I was amazed at the peaceful feeling I had about the whole thing. It was just a watch after all. True, I thought it was in the house someplace, but it could very easily have been thrown out in that trash bag or simply disappeared forever, who knows where. To me that experience and my response to it was a step forward toward the 5th dimension, i.e., letting go of material things.

The other thing that was really cool was that I got out of the habit of wearing my watch as I lived more and more in the moment, and things fell into place just fine without it, thank you very much. As a matter of fact, I slowed down in a lot of areas of my life, like taking my time at the grocery store enjoying the people and goodies all around me. Up to this point shopping was one of my very least favorite things to do. I found myself taking care of our home at my leisure, spending a lot of time enjoying nature around me. Oh yes, we still have clocks in the house for timing biscuits in the oven, arriving at a meeting on time, whatever is called for here in the 3rd dimension, but I seldom wear my watch. This was just a small opportunity for me to look at, to think about, and to realize a little bit of growth for me on my way to the 5th dimension. Remember, it's a gradual journey. As you proceed along your path you will find circumstances where something like this will come into play in your life as well, so it's important to be consciously aware of the changes taking place within you, and in your life, as you progress.

And it just keeps getting better, because without time there is no structure. Structure will dissipate as well. We human beings are not meant to be structured. Children diagnosed as ADD know this, and those diagnosed with Alzheimer's know it as well—they simply want to leave the structure of the 3rd dimension behind, and so they do. Personally, it has become more and more difficult to commit to things. I like to take them as they come. Don't ask me what I'm doing next week because I have no idea! Go with the flow, as they say. When you live in the moment, that's what happens, and everything always falls into place.

No borders, no barriers and no boundaries on anything. When you hear "no borders, barriers or boundaries" you naturally think about it in relationship to the different countries, different peoples and governments coming together, and that is what we are growing toward. But, think a little further. Think about living your life with no borders, no barriers and no boundaries. Think about being who you are and sharing that with the world with no borders, barriers or boundaries. Talk about freedom and flight of soul! Use your imagination, picture it, feel it, WOW!

With time non-existent, and no structure holding you in that tight little box that you've been afraid to jump out of, start imagining the freedom of living in the moment and just allowing things to unfold. I'm telling you, it's nothing but pure joy!

So, the 5th dimension is a place with opportunities to promote growth within ourselves of increased psychic awareness; the opening of the third eye; telepathic communication, our means of communication in the 5th dimension. This is all part of the 5th dimension.

The 5th dimension is a different learning arena with a different set of resources for us as we grow into the greater consciousness of God, and finally find and touch the face of God that we are.

The 5th dimension is definitely a place of more joy and more love than you can possibly imagine. It is a place of peace and serenity. You are free of fear, of guilt, of shame and you are free of the need to become anything in particular. You are simply at home with yourself.

Chapter 2

How Do I Start My Journey, or Have I?

Becoming more of who you are is your journey into the 5th dimension.

Moving into the 5th dimension is nothing more than changing your mind, making the decision to move out of the negative frequencies of the 3rd dimension, and closer to God's abundance in all areas of your life as you move forward into the 5th dimension. It's a matter of abiding in the greater truth of love, stepping from the 3rd and into the 5th, leaving behind the things of the 3rd dimension. The 3rd dimension still exists, but you are choosing to abide in truth and love, so it's a shift in consciousness that is taking place.

If you find joy in the little things in life, despite the chaos going on all around you—a new born baby, a little kitten or puppy, a beautiful sunset, a walk on the beach, so many things to enjoy and be thankful for—if you can find joy in the little things in spite the political crisis and general chaos of the world around you, if you can do this and at the same time find joy within yourself, you are well into your journey to the 5th dimension.

Have you noticed a change in how you respond to circumstances? Are you responding whereas you used to react? Are you less emotional, more compassionate, slower to judge, more prone to honesty, more willing to put more of yourself out there to the world? If your answer to these questions is "yes," then you are definitely on your way out of the 3rd and journeying toward the 5th dimension. If your answer is "no," then let's get started.

First of all it takes commitment, real commitment. Not a once in a while meditation, not a now and again chat with spirit, but a commitment to spend time every single day in meditation, in communion with God and spirit. I recommend that you have this quiet time at the same time and in the same place every day, if at all possible. This builds up the energy in the special place that you are creating during your meditation, providing an environment that is ready for you when you enter there, and carries you very quickly into your meditation.

I began my journey by studying the teachings of Jesus Christ that ultimately led me to the teachings of Dr. James Martin Peebles whose teachings are the same as those of Jesus Christ, but in a more down to earth language that is easier for human beings to understand. Every time Dr. Peebles comes through Summer Bacon during a public gathering he brings us an "Opening Statement" that always includes his three principles. These three principles when incorporated in tandem into our everyday life will lead us into the 5th dimension and beyond. Yes, I said "lead us" into the 5th dimension because you will find that as you bring these principles into your everyday life, the 3rd dimensional negative energies that hold us back, that keep messing up our lives one way or the other, will start to fall away as they are replaced by the lighter and more refined energies of the 5th dimension. So actually you will not be working to release the 3rd dimensional frequencies from you: they will naturally fall away in the process of bringing the three principles in tandem into your daily life.

The Three Principles are:

Number one: Loving allowance for all things to be in their own time and place, starting for yourself.

Number two: Increase communication with all of life, with respect.

Number three: Self responsibility for your life as a creative adventure, for through your choices and perceptions you do, indeed, create your own reality.

If you are not familiar with these three principles, I suggest that you write them down, memorize them, and practice using them in tandem in your daily life. I promise you they will change your life and carry you into the 5th dimension. It is up to you just how difficult your journey will be, depending upon how much you are willing to surrender to the journey, and how much you are willing to trust in God and the God that you are.

If you are already incorporating these three principles in your life—I mean really consciously doing your very best to live according to them—then you are already in the process of giving up the band of the 3rd dimensional lower frequencies, and moving on into the finer energy band of the 5th dimension.

Let's look at the first principle: *Loving allowance for all things to be in their own time and place, starting for yourself.*

Loving allowance for ALL things: that would include friends, family and others, animals, insects, plants, all living things, allowing them all to be (to be who and what they are) in their own time and place (not your time or place or anyone else's time or place, but their own time and place), and the most important part, and the most difficult for most of us, starting with yourself. Can you or do you have loving allowance for yourself? Are you allowing yourself to be who you are, and giving that to the world? Do you expect yourself to be perfect, or do you love yourself enough to know that you have always done the very best that you can in all situations; that if you could have done better you would have, and that every single word that you have spoken, every thought that you have ever had, every experience that you have had, everything in your life has brought you to where you are at this moment? Can you look back in retrospect, see that that is the case and be grateful for all of it, even though you may not be satisfied with where you are right now? You can either learn from your past and move forward, or you can begrudge your past and stay where you are. It's your choice.

One of the most common ways we humans have of not loving ourselves is in our self judgment. We are so good at judging ourselves, and not in a good way. And most of the time, that judging is in the form of comparing ourselves to others.

I have a wonderful group of friends that I met while taking classes and attending seminars as I continue learning more about spirituality. As it happened, in one particular group, everyone around me wanted to become a channel but me. I had absolutely no desire to become a channel. I kept wondering what I was doing in this group, why I was there. After all, I didn't want to become a channel, I just wanted to be the best healer I could be. They all did their homework, started channeling, doing all sorts of things, and there I was wondering why I wasn't moving forward as they were. What was wrong with me? I compared and compared and compared myself with them until finally (and this took at least four or five years) I discovered that I was indeed channeling all sorts of things as I was doing my healing work. I was receiving messages for my clients, I was being given the source of their discomfort, I was receiving help from other realms in my healing work and helping hundreds, maybe even thousands of stuck spirits go to the light. I was channeling and didn't even know it. Suddenly those years of judging myself, pretty harshly at times, thinking I was less than the others, thinking that something was wrong with me because I didn't want to become a channel, wondering what I was doing in this group, suddenly all of that disappeared. And again, here I am writing this book about the 5th dimension, filled with joy and excitement with who I am, and seeing once again that God does know my needs before I do. I did need to be with that group, I was doing my homework just as the others were, and I was channeling, it was just in a different way than the others. Yes indeed, life is good!

So if you are one who is prone to comparing yourself to others, stop! Stop now! Think about who you are, where you want to go, what you want to do, and remember that by your choices and perceptions you do indeed create your own reality, [This is the third principle but it fits here] so create your reality the way you want your reality to be, not someone else's idea of what that should be.

I knew I wanted to be there in that group, I knew I was where I needed to be, but I didn't know why. But I stuck with it, because it felt so right. So don't doubt what you feel. Don't doubt the choices you make when those choices come from your heart. Don't doubt what you feel inside, even when you don't understand that feeling. Go with it and trust yourself. Following your heart always works. Sometimes it's not easy, but only because we resist. It's our resistance to our truth that brings about the pain and discomfort.

I love the reality that I have created for myself by my choices and perceptions. True, a lot of my choices along the way gave me reason to doubt myself and my choices, but I stuck with them, and even though I may have doubted at times, deep down inside I knew they were right because they were straight from my heart and things fell into place. Maybe not always the way I thought they would or should, but always for my highest good.

One of the things I have found in having loving allowance for myself is that the old feelings of guilt that used to creep in if I felt I was letting someone down, or not doing something that I thought I should do (not doing my duty so to speak), those feelings of guilt have all gone. No more guilt trips. When you are living the three principles in tandem the very best that you can, there is never any reason to feel guilty about anything.

Another thing, when you start living with loving allowance for yourself in your life, you will, with certainty, discover that you have some very disgruntled family members and friends, especially the ones who have a tendency to want to control situations. They want to control everything and every one around them, including you. They think nothing of laying guilt trips on you to get you to do what they want you to do. I know that you know what I'm talking about here. Well, that's not going to work anymore now that you have loving allowance for yourself, and they won't like that very much. What works in the 3rd doesn't work in the 5th. Remember, people are afraid of what they don't understand, and they won't understand the change in you—why they can no longer control you so you just love them through it, through your growing and your movement into the 5th dimension. They will either fall away from you, and go their own way, or they will have loving allowance for you and stick around, or they will fall in love with what they see happening in your life and start their own journey, with you as their teacher and guide. You will also find that as some of your old friends drift away, others will be attracted to you. People of like mind and like heart will gravitate to you, and there you are with a circle of friends of like mind and like heart to enjoy and to share yourself with.

It takes a great deal of strength and courage to finally tell someone "no" when they ask something of you that you really don't want to do, when you have always told them "yes." Saying "no" in a gentle and loving way, and with compassion, does the job quite nicely. For instance: "You know, I really appreciate your kind offer, but I'm afraid that just doesn't fit my schedule right now, but thank you for thinking of me." You have shown loving allowance for yourself, and for the person asking the favor.

I was the greatest pushover ever, and it took me a long time to get to the place where I was able to say no. But believe me, it brings freedom like you can't even imagine. It's a matter of getting to a place where you are so happy with yourself that whatever other people think, do, or say about you doesn't matter, because you know who you are, and nothing anyone can do or say is going to change that.

We must keep ourselves the focus in the equation of our life. If there are things that we think we should do in order to be a good person, but those things are not a part of our dream or our passion, then it is not something that we need to do, but something that someone else needs to do in order to keep their focus and live their passion. In the past, as part of my comparing myself to others, I would look at all these wonderful volunteers who give their time to so many worthy causes and I would think to myself, "Gosh, they are doing so much for so many! I should be doing more." Then finally one day I looked around, took stock of the things that I do and realized, yes, I am giving to the world but in a different way, caring for the animals and birds around our home, volunteering healing and counseling to those who call, being there when someone needs someone who cares. We all have our own way of giving, and each one in a different way. It's all part of knowing who you are and carrying that with you at all times

*   *   *

When my husband and I moved to Arizona, we settled in one of the "spiritual centers" there. Being well into my "search for truth" by then, one of the first things I did was to look for a meditation group. I found a few, but none that suited me. You see, I just wanted to be with people of like mind and like heart and spend time meditating, going within and finding peace being with God and Spirit. No bells or whistles, no one taking center stage to talk about their conquests, just plain old meditating, communing with God and Spirit. I finally did find one, and it was wonderful, and after about a year the gal that lead the group decided to move on and turned it over to me. WHAT? ME? How in the world could I ever lead a meditation group? I was very quiet, very, very shy and one of the newest members of that group. Well . . . I DID IT! And there I was in the middle of another huge opportunity to grow.

What happened was, I started a group in our home. I shared with those that attended that it was a place to come and meditate in any way they wished. I didn't want anything that would interfere with anyone's quiet time with God and Spirit. There would be no bells or whistles, gongs, crystals, no grand standing, nothing to interfere with the quiet serenity of our surrender to and communion with God. Most understood and appreciated that, but there were some who did not. In order to keep my meditation group my meditation group I had to learn to say "no" and that took a lot of strength and courage on my part. Can you believe it? Forty years into my journey, and it still took all the courage I could gather to say "no" to someone, but that's how determined I was to have a meditation group where we could just meditate. So I said "no" to the person who wanted to bring singing crystal bowls. I said "no" to the person who wanted to Om. I said "no" to the person who wanted to bring chimes . . . and . . .

I had to call one member and ask that he not use our sharing time after our meditation to grandstand, to take over so to speak as teacher of the evening. Of course, some of those people stopped coming, but in the end we had a GREAT group! And for me . . . another giant step toward loving allowance for myself, increased communication and self responsibility for creating my own reality, and . . . the people that were unhappy with my group now had the opportunity to find a group that fit their needs, or to start a group of their own, to find and be with, and contribute to a group of like mind and like heart.

Through all of the changes that happen as a result of you stepping into your power keep remembering, "Loving allowance for all things to be in their own time and place (family and friends included), starting with yourself."

Interestingly enough, at this point I hadn't met Summer and Dr. Peebles, and didn't know about the Three Principles (or so I thought). You just never know how much Spirit is working with you, and through you. I did meet them shortly after this.

So now I'm studying the Three Principles, and applying them to my life as best I can, and bingo, God gives me yet another opportunity to make the Three Principles more a part of my life. By the way, the first time I heard Dr. Peebles give us his Three Principles I printed them out on my computer, framed them, and hung them on my wall above my computer, and memorized them. That was many years ago, and they are still there on the wall, and I am still working with them in tandem in my everyday life. Remember, this is a gradual journey.

By now I'm really into the study of Spiritual Healing, and clients are finding their way to my door. One such client was also a friend, a good friend who was working really hard on his path to heal not just physically, but spiritually as well. We talked a lot, and eventually he was calling me everyday for advice or simply to "dump," to share his disgruntlements with me. This went on for a few weeks until I realized that I was actually dreading getting out of bed in the morning, because I knew that I would receive that phone call and be bombarded with heavy negative energy. Oh boy, I was going to have to speak my truth to a good friend. Not only was it a very unpleasant way to start my day, but I had become his enabler, and that's not a good thing. I knew he would be angry but it was him or me, right? Right. So, I practiced what I would say, and prepared myself for all the scenarios I could think of, squeezed my eyes tight shut, gritted my teeth and waited for that fateful call.

It came right on schedule, and with a deep breath I spoke my truth and his as well. The situation was one where he kept going from healer to healer looking for someone to fix him, instead of going within and finding the source of his problems and starting there, healing from the inside out, the only way that really works. I expressed this truth to him gently, lovingly and very caring and sure enough, he became very angry, spoke very tersely, hung up and I didn't hear from him again. He was looking for a quick fix, for someone to do the healing for him, and that just doesn't work. I was speaking truth, his truth as well as my own. He was a great teacher for me because I was forced to speak our truth. His, so he could choose to move on or not, and mine, because I had to move on. I had to move on, and get out of a very depressing situation.

This is another example of using the Three Principles in tandem, loving allowance (for me, and for him as well), increased communication, and self responsibility for my life as a creative adventure: and, what an adventure it is.

*   *   *

As I got further into writing this book, I had what for me was an amazing experience, a feeling of complete and total freedom from responsibility for anyone but me. I don't remember ever having that feeling before.

I had the best sleep I've had in I can't remember when, and woke up feeling better than I've felt in I can't remember when. When I went to bed the night before, it was 9:00pm. I had made the decision within myself that "tonight will be just for me." I was going to bed because I was tired. My husband's foot hurt, but he would have to take care of that himself this time (I do a good deal of healing work for him), I prayed for no one in particular, thanked God for my abundance, and to bless the world and all living things, lay there, and just felt FREE. I was not taking care of anybody but me. I have never felt so free before. There was no guilt at all, and I think that was the difference. I wasn't taking care of anybody but me, and there was no guilt, no feeling of not doing the right thing, no feeling of not doing my duty.

I had released the 3rd dimensional energy of guilt, duty, and responsibility for others. It's like so many of us think that, because we are spiritual, because we are healers, because we are on our path so to speak, we think it's our duty to "save the world" and everyone in it when the "truth" is we are here to learn more about ourselves and our relationship with God, and the creator that we are, and in doing that and sharing ourselves with the world we do help to heal others in any way healing is needed. And, we do it naturally just by being who we are.

*   *   *

Giving your dreams up for someone else, because you feel it's your duty, is a very subtle thing. I mentioned in the short rundown of my life review, the loss of three businesses. These were businesses my husband wanted to pursue, and I went along in his support. After all, I'm his wife, I love him and it's my "duty," right? Right. My excitement in our ventures was for him, never for me. I really didn't like any part of it, but I wanted to, I chose to support my husband, because I love him very much, and I wanted him to be happy. Well . . . none of it worked. With my decision to support my husband because I do love him, I wasn't having any loving allowance for myself. I certainly wasn't speaking my truth through any of it, and I was creating a reality for myself that I really didn't want, and deep down inside I was not a very happy camper. I prayed and prayed that each business would be a success, and I was sincere in my prayers. My prayers were answered, just not in the way that I had in mind. Looking back, I can see that again, God knew my need before I did. The pain that I experienced through all of this was created by my resistance: resistance to loving allowance for myself, resistance to speaking my truth, resistance to creating the reality I wanted for me, resistance to following my heart.

Your greatest teachers are those closest to you. In this case it was my husband; I learned so much from our experiences during those years, and gained so much more than we lost.

I still get off track regarding people and circumstances I don't understand, and that's when I call up the three principles, work with them and eventually get back on track, and . . . remembering the feeling of being in the 5th dimension is a real catalyst for getting me through these challenges of the 3rd dimension as fast as possible.

It's a gradual process and there is always more.

The second principle: *Increase communication with all of life and with respect.*

The first principal is pretty self explanatory. The second principle took me a little longer to figure out. At first I thought it meant that I should be more outgoing, strike up a conversation with everyone I meet, be more of a people person, you know, someone who is always "on." Well, that's just not me. However, I am a very good listener: the other part of communication, and a very important part. It is so important to be a good listener. Being a good listener is being a good friend, a good companion, a healer, a counselor, as well as a really important part of being a parent. Yes, being a good listener plays a big part in increasing communication with all of life and with respect.

What happened in incorporating this second principle into my life, along with the first and third principles, was that I began to put more of myself out there, more of who I really am: the spiritual student, spiritual healer, spiritual counselor and teacher, and finally, spiritual writer. I've learned to share who I am with everyone I come into contact with. They ask, "What do you do?" and I respond, "Well I do a lot of healing and spiritual counseling, and right now I'm writing a book on the 5th dimension." I have really opened myself up to others, and the responses I get back from all of this are interesting, revealing, surprising, and a lot of fun, and opens up all kinds of communication with all kinds of people.

It was a long time coming though. There were so many years of being the odd one. Years of people not understanding or even wanting to know anything about spirituality; people shying away from me because of their fear of the unknown. This kind of response from people does tend to make you a little gun shy. But now, with me knowing who and what I am, and loving who and what I am, it's very easy to share who and what I am, knowing that whatever the response or reaction might be from others, it's not going to affect or change who or what I am in any way.

You see, truth is truth: it never changes. People can doubt it, argue it, make fun or call it a lie. They can believe anything they like, but the truth remains the truth no matter what. So in knowing the truth of me, nothing anyone can ever say or do will change that. So, part of my "increasing communication with respect," is in my putting myself out there as I am. So, go ahead, know the truth of you and share it with the world. It's really fun.

There's more. Open yourself up to everything and everyone, you just never know what you might find. It's so much fun, changing a frown to a smile because you smile, and say "hi" to someone in the grocery store. You don't even have to say "hi" if you don't want to. Just a smile will do wonders for someone. It could very well turn the whole day around for that person, i.e., the look on the clerk's face when you say, "thank you," again, with a smile. Smiles are so contagious, and they're free! I've had a lot of fun just walking through a mall or down the street and saying "hi" with a smile to a stranger. Some may think I'm crazy, but that's okay. The ones that change their frown to a smile more than make up for it. It's just plain fun seeing the different reactions from people. Don't forget, we are all children of God, and we all have that spark of light within us, and you never know how, with just a smile, a kind deed, or a cheery word, how you may spark that light within someone and lighten up their soul just a little bit more. And, I bet, because of your willingness to share yourself with the world in such a beautiful way, I bet they will pay it forward and do the same for someone else. These are easy things to do while increasing communication with all of life with respect, and so rewarding.

So many relationships are ruined by lack of communication. Everyone thinks everyone is a mind reader. Guess what? They're not! You need to communicate! Communicate and communicate some more. It's not an easy thing to do for most people, but so important. Be honest and up front with your loved ones, with everyone in your life. It doesn't have to be confrontational, or bitter, or yelling and screaming. That's not communication: that's expressing anger, hurt, and disappointment from lack of communication. Remember, it's increased communication, with respect.

If you have pets, I'm sure you communicate with them. How about animals who are not your pets? How about critters? How about trees? How about all of life? Sound silly, or maybe even crazy? Not at all. We are surrounded by so much beautiful life. It's all alive, and it's all communicating with us one way or another. We can learn so much if we take the time to listen and to observe.

We have so many birds around our home, it's like living in the middle of an Aviary. It's wonderful, and yes, I communicate with them constantly. Have you ever watched a bird build its nest? Talk about patience and focus, and the result of their patience and focus is unbelievable. The intricacy and strength of the nest is over the top. We had a bird build his nest in our Maple tree in our back yard last year, and that nest is still there. It has survived Monsoon downpours and gale strength winds, and it is still there. The birds are back this year, but have built a new nest, same tree, new nest.

Critters? Well, have you ever tried telling a spider that you would really rather have it make its home outside of your house instead of inside? Try it. You may be surprised. When we see a critter or a creepy crawler, our first thought is to squash it. Please don't. Instead, remember the first principle, loving allowance for all things to be. Guide the fly outside. Put that tiny bug outside where it can get something to eat. Do what you can to help it along its way as you use these principles in tandem in your everyday life.

And, how about communication with yourself? How can you know what's going on with you, if you don't communicate with your self? That's what you're doing when you go within; you're making contact with self, asking questions of self, and LISTENING for answers from self, from that still small voice from within that is you. Oh yes, some say that's spirit with the answers, that's "God leading me." Well . . . guess what? That's that still small voice within: that's you! That's the source of you. Remember, "if you have the question, you have the answer." That is you: the one who knows what is the very best for you, so listen, really listen, and trust what you hear.

Yes, communication with all of life with respect is fun, rewarding, expansive and brings a lot of richness into our lives.

And the third principle: *Self responsibility for your life as a creative adventure, for through YOUR choices and perceptions you do, indeed, create your own reality.*

Well, there you have it. So it's time to stop blaming God, to stop blaming our parents, our siblings, the world conditions, whoever or whatever it is that in the past we have blamed for what we considered to be the bad stuff in our lives, and to start embracing the fact that we do indeed create our own reality. And if you are a student of the Bible how about:

" . . . whatsoever a man soweth, that shall he also reap."
(Galatians 6:7)

or if you don't happen to be into the Bible, how about this one that I'm sure you are familiar with:

"What goes around comes around."

There are a lot of different ways to say the same thing.

Once you embrace this concept, your movement forward will take off like crazy. Blaming others just doesn't work, and keeps you stuck. You do indeed create your own reality by every word, every deed, every thought you have ever had. So, if you want things to change in your life, you are the only one that can create that change. And yes, I'm still being given lessons, opportunities to learn more about what I'm talking about here (those little pebbles in the path) to share with you as I write.

For instance:

I received one of my monthly bills today, opened it up and immediately jumped into fear. Expecting a bill for around $35, the Total Due was for $201.95! There it was big as life, under "Other Charges & Credits" $166.97, no other explanation other than the "Other Charges & Credits" which, when added to the rest of the bill totaled $201.95. Within seconds I was on the phone asking for an explanation, got the usual contact that was just doing his job and no way would he let me go beyond him to a higher authority. It all had to do with something that I had returned three months previous and they showed no record of receiving the item. Well, we went back and forth and back and forth, and here I am, back in the 3rd dimension, ranting and raving, inviting in a huge headache, and not being very nice to the person on the other end of the line who was just doing his job. They could not and would not do anything until they tracked down the item. They offered to arrange a payment plan for me to pay it off. All the time I was in this 3rd dimensional mode telling him, "I'm not paying. I don't care if they cut off my service. They can do whatever they want. I returned the product and I'm not paying for something that's not my doing. I did the right thing from my end and no way am I going to pay for someone else's screw up."

Luckily I am a person who keeps records. Can't always find them on the spot, but eventually I did find the paperwork and receipt from the shipping company that I had used, gave the people in question here all the numbers, and my account was credited for the full amount of the "Other Charges & Credits."

In retrospect, I see how easy it is to slip into the lower frequency band of the 3rd dimension. And, just look at the energy I let loose in the world. That energy goes out there and stays. I added so much anger and frustration to the world, and there is no way to call it back. I tell you what though: in looking back at this whole thing, what a beautiful lesson in how easy it is to slip, and to see what you give to the world in anger and frustration during situations like this. There was no loving allowance here. I did increase communication, but not in a good way, and I'm certainly not proud of what I created in my own reality.

I did apologize to the young man who was just doing his job and had put up with my anger during this whole fiasco.

This idea of creating your own reality is not a very easy thing to embrace. It means taking responsibility for your life as it is today. Again, everything you have ever said or done, every thought you have ever had, every decision you have ever made, have made your life what it is today, and your thoughts, words and deeds of today are creating your tomorrow. So pay attention: be aware of what you are creating for yourself.

What you experience is not his fault, her fault, their fault, God's fault, Spirit's fault, not anyone else's fault. What you experience is the result of your choices and perceptions. And there really isn't any fault here at all. Whatever the experience, it just is what it is, not good, not bad, it just is. And whatever it is it's there for you to look at and to experience, to examine it and learn from it. There is always something to learn from any experience, and if that experience involves more than just you, then there is something in that experience for everyone involved in that experience to learn. Remember we are all in this together.

Experiences that you consider bad are not bad at all, they are opportunities. Now don't laugh or do that "yeah right" thing. This is just more truth. We create these situations to learn from. We're here to learn, so take advantage of these seemingly painful and uncomfortable situations and learn from them.

I reached a point where I could look at these "uncomfortable and painful" situations, wonder what "this" was about, dive into that situation all the way with both feet, experience the "darker spaces" as they're called, wallow in it for a while: I mean really wallow in it. The more I wallowed, the faster I came out the other end, a little lighter than before, excited about what I had learned in the process, rested a while, and waited for the next lesson I needed to learn to move me along my path. It works. It got to be a game. Look at it straight in the eye and give it all you've got. May as well get it over with and go on to the next "learning opportunity." You will shorten your journey quite a bit this way until you stop resisting, and start allowing.

Once you learn to allow, you are entering the 5th dimension because all of your 3rd dimensional fears are dissipating along the way, and your journey can continue without pain. You may still have those little pebbles as you move along your path, but now you are allowing, not resisting, and that takes away the pain.

*   *   *

Do you have yourself trapped in a box? There is always more, and so staying in a box just doesn't work and won't work in the 5ᵗʰ Dimension. How can you grow if you keep yourself in a box with those borders, barriers and boundaries?

I started out with wanting to know about healing the way Jesus Christ healed. That led me to a class in Triom, a little known but very profound healing method. From there I went to Reiki, but there is always more. Jumping out of the box and away from the rules of Reiki my next step was remote healing as I learned to surrender more and more to love, allowing love to flow freely through me. Still learning to surrender to God and all that is, the next thing I knew I was toning: an even more profound way of healing. Toning is about surrendering to 'what is', being in the moment with all that is, and allowing whatever energies are called for to have full and free use of all that I am. During this time I spent four years training with Archangel Gabriel every morning for from 1-1/2 to 2 hours laying on the floor in my special meditation room learning to surrender, surrender, surrender. So you see, this process didn't exactly happen overnight. I'm not the fastest learner in the world, but I am tenacious when it comes to my journey here.

There is always more, and if we keep ourselves in a box, if we don't allow ourselves to keep moving forward, to get out there and stretch ourselves as far as we can, then we stagnate just as the water in a stream stagnates once it gets out of the flow of it's source.

Every one of the experiences we have along the way is important, as well as the tools that we use to keep us moving forward, to help us in our expansion into more and more of who we really are. They are very important as long as we keep moving and don't allow ourselves to get trapped in those experiences or the tools. Reiki, Triom, crystals, singing bowls, healing with color, teachers, Gurus, whatever the case may be, these are all tools there to help us. But, if we get stuck in any of these tools, then we are stuck, we are in a box, we are not moving forward but stagnating. Learn from the tool, and when you have learned what you are there to learn, be willing to move on because . . . there is always more.

Chapter 3

YOU CAN JOURNEY WITHOUT PAIN

Life is meant to be lived, without pain. It really is. It's not a necessity to have pain in order to have growth.

It's a given that our Planet Earth is on her way to the 5th dimension, and you can make the journey without pain should you choose to make the journey with her. You can make any part of your journey in this incarnation without pain. Yes, you can. Before we start our journey here, I would like you to understand this: life is meant to be lived without pain. The pain comes from our resistance to our journey, our resistance to life. The pain, discomfort, those things that to us seem so difficult to deal with, all of that comes from our resistance, our resistance to who we are, our resistance to seeing life as an ongoing learning experience. You know, if you would look at every situation that comes your way and ask yourself what this is all about, what is here for you to learn, and see it for what it is, then delve into the situation without fear because you know that when you come out the other side you will be lighter. You will have grown and moved forward on your path without the pain, the poor me's, and all of the miseries that we create for ourselves through our resistance. Once you adopt this attitude you will find that it speeds up your journey back to God, and you actually look forward to your next challenge to delve into, learn, and move forward again. You can make it a game: a game without pain.

This doesn't necessarily mean it's fun, but it's not painful! I've done it. I've been through enough of those "learning opportunities" to know that when one comes along, there is something more I have to learn: you know, a little pebble or a rock or maybe even a bolder in your path to deal with.

I delve into it with both feet, wallow for as long as it takes for me to "get it," and come out the other end a little bit lighter, a little bit more loving, and with more understanding of life around me than before, ready to go about my business, happy in knowing that I'm just a little bit further along my path, (or maybe a lot further along on my path than I was before that "learning opportunity"), knowing that, just like the 'ol bus, there's another "learning opportunity" on it's way, because the learning never ends, there's always more.

In every situation, you have a choice. When the choice is a particularly difficult one to make, stop and listen to that still small voice within you. In your imagination, put yourself in both situations. Which one feels the best? You'll know. Your tummy will tell you. It knots up when considering the decision not in your best interest. I used to tell our children this when they were growing up. They couldn't argue the wisdom in it. Whenever they went against that still small voice within, whenever they went ahead even though their tummy was saying "no," good things did not happen.

A quote from Dr. Peebles tells us, "The flower is not screaming out in pain as it is opening." The flower starts its journey as a tiny little seed planted in the dark and fertile soil. It slowly works it's way up through the soil, making it's way around or pushing aside the little pebbles and rocks that get in the way, having no idea what its purpose is, what's in store for it, not questioning, not whining, just making it's way out of the dark and fertile soil and out into the light where it opens into a beautiful perfect flower bringing joy and beauty to share with the world.

So keep in mind that it is our resistance to the lessons that we create (to learn whatever it is that we are here to learn) that cause the stress, the pain, and slows down our progress. The circumstances are not painful. They just are what they are. It is our resistance to them that causes the pain.

Chapter 4

WELCOME TO YOUR JOURNEY TO THE 5TH DIMENSION: PREPARING PHYSICALLY, MENTALLY, EMOTIONALLY AND SPIRITUALLY FOR YOUR JOURNEY

GET HEALTHY! Your body is being jolted by the changes going on in the world. The downturn of our economy and the changes going on within our government are taking a huge toll on our emotional bodies, which in turn taxes our physical bodies to the max. Not only that, but our DNA is changing as well. Yes . . . it's true, our DNA is changing. Again, and you will hear this throughout the book, don't forget that this is a gradual journey we are on.

Be sure you get plenty of rest. You'll need it. Your body will be going through profound changes. Listen to that still small voice within. Some call it your intuition. Your body will tell you what it needs. Eat healthy, and rest when your body asks for it. There will be times when all you can do is rest. There are things you want to do, things you think have to be done, and your body is screaming out, "Please, please lay down! I am just so tired I can hardly move, I can barely put one foot in front of the other!" Best you listen and lay down, not necessarily for an hour or so, but twenty or thirty minutes will do. Spirit works with you a lot while you are sleeping at night. If a lot of work has been done with you and/or through you during your sleep time, then your body will be tired and will need time to catch up. Try not to push yourself. When you do, that's when good old Mother Nature comes along. Well, really not Mother Nature, but that part of you that knows you need rest, and knocks you out with a cold, the flu, or whatever, and then you have no choice, there you are, in bed, resting after all.

Allow some time for exercise. It doesn't have to be world-class exercise. A little stretching, a little bending and some walking does wonders.

And while we're on the subject of our physical body, try talking to it, letting your body know how much you appreciate it. You'll be surprised at how much better it will respond to your needs. Everything is God, and that includes every cell of our body. Each cell has its own intelligence, and each cell works together with the other cells throughout our body. Consequently, when one cell or one section of our body shuts down, all other areas of our body are affected. We've got the "As above, so below" or the "Macro/Micro" going on here. I look at it as this: we are to the cells of our body as God is to us, so we need to take care of our body as God takes care of us. We all love a little pat on the back and feel much better for it don't we? So why not do the same for our body by showing our appreciation for it?

Thank your body for whatever service it has done for you. Whether it be a perfect or imperfect body, doesn't matter: it's the one you chose when you came into this incarnation to serve you, and it is serving you perfectly. Even though you may not think so, it is.

I can't talk about taking care of your physicality without mentioning the influence the media has on the health of the masses. Turn off, or at least mute the TV, radio, and the internet when the commercials for drugs and news of so called epidemics come on. As strong and knowing as you may be, some of those negative thoughts being projected out from the media might just find a way into your consciousness. You can't afford to buy into anything they're trying to sell you. You know that as soon as one person has a symptom that no one can describe, a name is put to it, a drug is found for it, and pretty soon there's an epidemic. Don't allow yourself to slip into that equation.

With that said, start toning. Use toning vibrations to bring healing and more health into your physical body for these new adjustments that your new position in the 5th dimension demand. I recommend toning because it is powerful, and simple, and the most profound healing tool I have experienced to date, and it is a self healing tool. Any modality of healing used here in the 3rd dimension will help you through your transition to the 5th dimension to a point. However, with the toning you are able to go much deeper within self, and communicate directly with Spirit through your toning.

[If you are not familiar with toning then I suggest you visit my web site at *http://simplespirituality.net*.

Most important of all, remember always to love and to appreciate your physical body.

PREPARE THE MIND AND THE EMOTIONAL BODY

One of the things that may happen should you decide to continue your journey into the 5th dimension is that you may find some of your family and friends drifting away. It happens. They don't understand what's going on with you. You have fewer and fewer things in common. It becomes more and more awkward being together trying to carry on a conversation. A common reason for this drifting away is that the people who used to be able to control you are not able to control you any longer, because you have stepped into your own power, and they just can't handle that. So prepare yourself for the possible drifting away of some of your friends, and maybe even some members of your family.

I think that's one of the first things I noticed: people falling away from me. I was different, I was weird, I was spiritual, I must be crazy so people started falling away. Some of my "friends" who thought I was so wonderful in the beginning of my journey, stopped coming around once I started saying "no" to their requests for favors having stepped into my power to a small degree back then.

Back then, we were living in our first home, where we lived for twenty-three years. It was a new housing development. All of the homeowners were about the same age, and all with children the same age as ours. What an experience that was! We had many wonderful times, and at the same time it was an enormously challenging time for me with more opportunities for growth than I can count.

There was a small group of us who would get together regularly to play cards or just socialize in general. On one of these occasions we were all talking about places we would like to visit, and my dream had always been to visit Egypt. I had read book after book on Egypt, most of them authored by R.A. and Isha Schwaller De Lubicz, husband and wife who spent 15 years in the study of the art and architecture of the Temple of Luxor in Egypt. Their books were filled with ancient Egyptian philosophy, spirituality, mathematics and how the temples there were built according to

the same dimensions of man, and all with such deep spiritual meanings . . .
well . . . it rocked my world. I thought it was absolutely fascinating.

So, when I shared with the group that my dream had always been to
go to Egypt, and that I was actually going to live my dream and visit the
Pyramids, the temples, and see the Sphinx, they couldn't understand why.
And as I tried to explain why, and in so doing revealed the spiritual side of
me, you could have heard a pin drop as their mouths dropped to the floor. I
guess they didn't know how to handle the spiritual part of me. It had never
come up, never been a reason for it to. Well, needless to say, my involvement
in the group became less and less until poof . . . it was no more.

(I don't know though. You know, sometimes it's kind of fun to watch
people's mouths drop to the floor . . . ooops, now would that be considered
3rd or 5th dimensional?)

Part of preparing the mind is to know with every ounce of your being
how very important you are to all that is, to the world, the Universe, to all
that is, was, and ever shall be.

You think that you don't count, that you don't make a difference,
that you're not important, well think again. You do count, you do make a
difference, you are important!

This may come as a surprise to you, but everything that you do, everything
that you say, every conscious thought that you have, even every unconscious
thought that you have affects not only you, but everyone around you. It
affects all things: yes, all things, and can you guess why? Because everything
is energy/frequency. Our energy/frequencies are constantly emanating out
from us, as we are all in the oneness together. Anything else is illusion.

If you doubt this, then think about the different feelings you get around
different people. So here we are again living in our first home with three
small children, back in the days when the men went off to work, and the
women stayed home to take care of the house and look after the children.
And later, when the children were in school, there were coffee klatches: you
know, go have coffee with the neighbors and chat, plan get togethers, with
a little gossip thrown in, as I recall.

Well, there was one particular neighbor that I would visit. She was a very
nice person, and she really liked to talk, and it was all good (or so it seemed)
until one day I suddenly realized how depressed I was after every visit with
her. I don't believe she had a positive word or thought within her. She was
a very unhappy person. I knew for my own sake that I had to stop going
over there, and as difficult as it was for me to do, I did it. I stopped visiting
her, and in doing that I took one giant step into my own power, and I did

it using the Three Principals in tandem. In doing it I had loving allowance for myself, I increased communication with her with respect, and I created a much better reality for myself. Of course, back then I didn't know about the Three Principles. I didn't meet Summer and Dr. Peebles until forty years later, but I did know the teachings of Jesus Christ.

That's how energy works: we are all interconnected, our energies going out from us in all directions, interacting with all the other energies going out from everyone and everything around us.

Think of it this way: picture a spider standing on its web and gyrating, and the web is feeling all the vibrations from the spider, and the spider (that is you, you are the spider) is at the center of the web of consciousness. Now visualize this web of consciousness with many spiders on it, many spiders dancing, gyrating in different motions all interconnected within this web, all at the same time, being affected by one another on this web of consciousness.

It's a beautiful dance, it is a resonance, it is a radiation of humanity one towards the other. Now you can see how every conscious thought and every unconscious thought does gyrate and dance and radiate out into the Universe and have an effect. Sometimes we believe that we do not have an effect in the world, but in truth we do: with every breath that we take, every move that we make, every decision, every choice, every perception, as we create our reality that we are sharing with the world.

PREPARE YOUR SPIRITUAL BODY

Incorporate the "Three Principles" in tandem daily in your life.

Chapter 5

CHECK POINT TRUST: WHERE DO YOU PUT YOURS?

Learn to trust yourself, your insights, your intuition, learn to trust God, The Source, the Universe, The Oneness, whatever you choose to call it. Ask yourself what it is you are putting your trust in.

We live in a world based in fear, not love. We are constantly bombarded with negativity by the media. They tell us it's flu season, it sinks into our consciousness and the next thing you know, everyone has the flu. A doctor sees a patient that they can't diagnose, they give this new condition a name, shout it to the world and bingo . . . we have an epidemic of what was unknown just a short while ago.

Granted, it takes an awful lot of faith to know that these frequencies of flu, colds, cancer, Alzheimer's and all the rest aren't going to get you, but remember, it is a gradual journey and you have plenty of time to practice, to look at, and to discover where your trust lies. Does it lie in that pill, in that shot, in what everyone is telling you to believe? Or does your trust lie within you, within your heart, in what you know to be true? Does your trust lie in your truth?

Now, I'm not saying to go out and cancel all your insurance policies or throw away you medications. I'm just giving you some idea of how subtle these issues are.

I know what you're thinking: what about those who came into this incarnation with existing disabilities? Well, those human beings chose to come into this incarnation in that particular way in order to teach the rest of us about love, about compassion, to appreciate life, and they chose to come in that way in order for them to learn whatever it is they themselves are here to learn.

"The only way our planet is going to make it through these difficult times is by bringing more compassion to it."

Some of you may know about "The Elephant Man," John Merrick. There is a movie about his life titled "The Elephant Man." This was the sweetest, purest and most compassionate person you can imagine. He was so disfigured that his mother gave him up when he was a very small child. He was horribly abused, presented as a freak in sideshows, humiliated, beaten, degraded at every turn and yet his love for God never waivered nor did his love for humanity.

I am very fortunate to have been present at a channeling of John Merrick by a very clear and real channel a while back. I would like to share here what he said at that channeling:

Question: Is this John Merrick?

John: Indeed I am John, and I certainly have been waiting an awfully long time to speak to you beautiful souls, to express to you that the flesh is such a limited expression of the soul and not to be taken so seriously.

And I certainly experienced ecstasy of an existence and life within a shell. I was still able to experience the glory of life upon your planet in a fashion of my own design, to be apart, yet one, and to experience the ecstasy of life, the joy of my creation, and to love those around me who were not able to see beyond my shape, as they are the ones in the dark, not I.

I was able to share of compassion with the world as I would not had been able to share in any other skin, and it was a gift from me to the earth and the earth to me as I realized my God self upon the planet earth. The pain was my joy, and the joy was my pain, and my altruism was my solace as I found my way into the arms of our Lord in a love that is beyond words, as you understand. Those in this room, you understand. The beauty of our souls, the magnitude of the love God has shown us all.

I have found myself in God, as you all will in time. And it is a beauty and a joy, a beauty and a joy, and I share with you MY LOVE, all creation, existence, your reality, in this room today, each and every one of you such beauty, such priceless joy.

Do you understand the light that you are, you have been and that you will be? I am overwhelmed by the beauty of the light in the room today, and I've not been able to transport myself back to the planet earth before. I see all kindred spirits, beyond time, beyond space. It's here. My love, my joy, MY LOVE, MY JOY I share with you, I impart to you, I fill your souls with my love and your light shines upon me and raises me and exalts me.

I honor you in this room today. I honor you in this room today. I honor you in this room today.

John Merrick chose to come into that particular lifetime with a congenital disorder that eventually caused this physical disfigurement.

His love and compassion radiated from every word he spoke in that room that day, soft, gentle and embracing.

Chapter 6

THE JOURNEY

If you have made the decision to move forward, then you are already in the movement toward the 5th dimension: it is happening inside of you. The reflection of that in your life can be seen as you start claiming your truth more than ever before. You will feel clear in your thoughts in insecure times. You will start having more vivid dreams. In your daytime imaginings you will wonder if they are imaginings or are they real. You will experience a sort of blurring as to what is real and what is not as you start seeing into other dimensions. You will see shapes and figures, size and colors that you have not experienced before here on Planet Earth.

These are some of the things you may experience during your journey, but don't put these things into a box by expecting great things out of your movement into the 5th dimension, by getting stuck in your expectations, because the bottom line is that the 5th dimension is simply another way to look at the world without incorporating time and space, and it is our journey there that counts. Our growth, our expansion is in the journey, not in the destination.

To help you along on your journey into the 5th dimension, situations will occur to show you how you are progressing, situations that in the past have caused negative reactions within you. In the past you looked at these situations. You went within and found the cause of your reaction to that situation, and you worked with the cause. You think you have released whatever thought pattern caused your reaction to that situation, and you replaced that thought pattern with unconditional love. The jealousy, greed, prejudice, low self esteem, whatever the cause may have been, you truly believe that you have taken care of it and then, without warning, there you are being presented with a situation that brings up that same reaction as before, the cause of which you had worked with so hard; the cause that you thought you had conquered and replaced with unconditional love. Well, a little disheartening I grant you, but it's exactly what we need to show us how we're doing. A reality check, I guess you could call it. These situations will continue to show up until one day we are confronted with a similar situation, and we don't react . . . we respond with loving allowance, increased communication and self responsibility.

You will become more sensitive to everything; you senses will be more finely tuned. Be aware of you, be aware of what you see, what you hear, how you respond to situations in your life. Your vision will become much finer, you will start to see air, energy, colors you have never seen before. Taste buds will be more sensitive as your energy/frequencies become more and more finely attuned.

There will be physical changes as well, one of the most profound; your DNA is changing, so start being aware of YOU.

Let's talk about love, sympathy and compassion, because your feelings will change here as well. When you say you love someone, can you replace the word "love" with "compassion" and say that you have compassion for that person?

One of the first things I noticed changing within me was that I was crying less as my acceptance of "it is what it is" increased. I was afraid that I was becoming less caring, but I knew that wasn't the case. I still have deep, very deep, compassion for people, animals, every living thing, but I am understanding more and more that everything is as it should be, regardless of how things appear. I have learned this through many difficult situations of my own (those learning opportunities we've been talking about here), and also thinking a lot about how Jesus Christ, Dr. Peebles and our guides do all they can to help us. But, in that process they do not solve our problems for us, they do not feel sorry for us, but have great compassion for us, so much so that they can stand back and allow us to go through whatever we set ourselves up to go through in order for us to learn whatever it is we came here to learn. That's loving allowance with compassion. No pity or "feeling sorry" for us, just a lot of compassion. It takes great courage for us to do the same, and that's why it is so important to learn and to embrace "it is what it is." No good, no bad, no judgment: it just "is what it is".

When we feel sympathy for someone, we have a tendency to get involved with their negative energy field, feeling sorry for them, becoming their enabler, adding our energy to their energy that is feeding the cause of whatever it is that is creating the circumstance. When we do this, we are not helping them in any way, but "enabling" them to stay where they are instead of helping them to work their way out of the situation. Yes, we do become their enabler. To love this person with compassion is to allow them to work through their challenge supporting them in any and every way that we can. Some call this "tough love," and I don't know who it's toughest on: the challenged or the one trying to help, especially when dealing with those closest to you.

Far better to feel compassion for them as you love them, help them, pray for them, but not join them in giving your energy to the circumstance. We have all been in this kind of a situation, and it's not easy. It's so easy to get caught up in the problems of everyone around you: the world situation, everything that is going on. It's so easy to get caught up in it, and before you know it you're depressed, beating yourself up for the slightest little thing, wondering what happened to that "freedom and flight of soul" feeling you had just a little while ago. So, always be aware: feel compassion for everything and everyone, know that everything is in right order and relax, release, and surrender, and keep working with the Three Principles.

Your capacity for compassion for others will increase with your frequency change as you better understand why others act as they do. You'll understand that everyone is in pain of one kind or another, and that they are doing the best that they can. You'll love them and have compassion for them, but you can't fix them. Be at peace with that. Be at peace with knowing that they are the only ones who can do the fixing, that it's their choice to fix themselves or not, and that they are creating their reality.

I know that I have been judged as cold and uncaring in the past by some, but later on down the line these same people have come to me with love, understanding and a lot of gratitude for my honesty in helping them through difficult (and, to them, very painful) situations. It's another circumstance of standing in your truth no matter what. Instead of being in sympathy with a person and allowing them to stay in that place of "pity poor me," you let them know how much you love them, and you support them with suggestions of what is really going on in their life at that moment, and what might be done to pull them out of that place.

I have seen people totally turn around when I have, with their permission, shared with them things that I have seen and felt going on within them that they were totally unaware of themselves. When you are standing on the outside of a situation you can see it much more clearly than those who are going through it. But, it must be shared with compassion, understanding, caring and a lot of love.

I do a lot of healing and counseling, and if I sugar coated some of the things that I pick up during these sessions I would be cheating the client. I share it all with love and compassion, of course, but also with honesty, and they appreciate that. They usually laugh a little, tell me I'm absolutely right, then deal with the problem and move on with their life.

If you start feeling that you are becoming less loving and caring, you're not. The reality is that you are becoming more compassionate, more understanding and aware of what is real and what is illusion.

Think about your guides, think about God. We do not always receive what we ask for, and our guides don't always step in to help us out of our challenges. No, they watch over us, they love us and have such deep compassion for us it's impossible for us to even imagine the magnitude of that love. They stand back and allow us to experience what they know we need to experience in order for us to learn whatever it is we need to learn. There's that tough love again.

Do things that you once found interesting and exciting now bore you?

You may find that your enthusiasm about things 3rd dimensional diminishes as you move forward into the 5th dimension of the finer and lighter frequencies of love, more interesting things, new things, amazing things.

I asked the question, "What happened to my passion of becoming the best healer I could become?"

My passion and primary focus for years has been to become as much like Jesus Christ as possible, and to realize this through spiritual healing. I studied all forms of hands on healing, investigating color, crystals, meridians, Tai Ji, Reiki, Quantum Healing. You name it; I investigated it. In the end, what I found, what worked for me, was to keep it simple and let God do the work through me. I went from hands on healing, to remote healing, just bringing the client into my consciousness and allowing whatever needed to take place to take place; removing myself completely from the situation and allowing spirit to take over. It was beautiful and incredibly exciting for me.

All of this progressed over time and I imagined that this would be my life. Well, no. Life just keeps going on, and the lessons keep coming, and we keep moving closer and closer to God, to the Oneness, Universal love, that which holds everything together, whatever that is for you, realizing more and more who and what we really are; moving into the knowledge of our oneness with all things, the knowledge that we are light, that we are love, that we are the creator of who we are.

I was really very happy with the way things were going, and then one day all of this changed. I was still happy, of course, but I found that instead of the prayer, the meditation, the using of whatever words came through in the process of communication with all that is, all of a sudden I found myself toning. It was amazing, I was absolutely blown away. No words, just this wonderful communication with all that is through toning. Now I was passionate about healing through toning. I wrote a book and created a CD all about toning to share with anyone and everyone the amazing power of toning. It opens you up as never before, and starts you on your journey into the 5th dimension by taking you deep within yourself, and in that process starts you on your way in the replacing of the 3rd dimensional emotional baggage you are carrying as a result of your experiences here, and replacing it with love: love of self, and love of all things, things of the 5th dimension. So, yes, there is always more, the journey never ends. This is what I, and many, many others experience in the toning process.

The more I tone the deeper I go within myself, the more I am at peace with everyone and everything, knowing—really knowing—that "it is what it is," and understanding that nothing matters and yet everything matters.

Then one day I realized that I was slowing down. I was doing more and more things that I felt I didn't have time for before. I was spending more time on the phone with family and friends, gardening when I felt like it, with no regard to the fact that I hadn't spent time that morning meditating. I was grocery shopping, something I had never taken time to enjoy before, feeling that I had better things to do. What I found as I was slowing down and taking the time to do these things, things that I had thought in the past living in my structured world I didn't have time for, I found I was enjoying more and more of the things around me, enjoying all of life as it presented itself to me.

Oh my goodness, am I falling away from spirit? Am I losing my passion for healing by spending more time on other things? What's going on here? Then, BINGO, yes! I am enjoying more of myself, more of who I am, allowing more of myself to come into play. I'm learning more about me being the center of my Universe, and that it's all about me, without guilt: the guilt that used to come into play when not doing the things that I felt were my duty to do. What a feeling! It's the freedom and flight of soul we hear so much about. It's all about, "What God wants from you is you."

I still do as much meditating, as much healing and toning, as much counseling as ever, but I am doing all of that without structure, without those borders, barriers and boundaries that keep us in that tight little box of ours.

And now it was happening again! I was bored. I had done hands on healing, remote healing, channeling and finally toning. I had found answers to burning questions. Now what? I didn't understand any of this. I couldn't understand why I was feeling bored after being so excited with my healing work and the profundity of it. Again, I felt like I was slipping away from Spirit, like I was floundering, not realizing that there was something more, that it was time for something new, time to move on, but I had no idea what that could possibly be. And then spirit stepped in and said write a book on the 5th dimension. Yea! Something more to learn! Another area to grow in! Something I know absolutely nothing about, and, oh my gosh, is so much fun learning.

Now don't misunderstand: I still love healing, whether it's hands on, remote or toning. I still love doing all of those things, but it's like you don't want to stay in the same grade in school semester after semester, you want to keep learning more, expanding more, taking with you what you have learned and adding to it, becoming more and more of who you are.

So, you see, there is always more, the learning never ends. When you hit one of those "dry grass periods" where you find yourself becoming bored and losing interest in the things that used to fulfill you in the 3rd dimension just wait, relax, release and surrender to whatever is coming your way.

*   *   *

As I said in the beginning of this book, my life review continues for me as I write. As the different learning experiences play out in front of me, I share those that I think may be of help to you. It's really interesting. It's like one last go 'round, to look at them, embrace them and then leave them behind as I work my way toward the 5th dimension.

This will happen and is happening to you as well: it's part of the journey to the 5th dimension. You will eventually find yourself in a "life" review, and it will help you to know how far you have come on your journey.

It was 4:00 a.m., and I couldn't sleep. When that happens, I go into my meditation room and spend time with Dr. Peebles, Gabriel, and John. I discuss the book with Dr. Peebles and totally relax in the love of Gabriel and John. They are just so easy to be with. I started thinking about the 5th

dimension, and the fact that time disappears there. I have, during the writing of this book, spent time there where time does not exist, and it's wonderful. There is absolutely no way to describe the feeling. It's so freeing. I mean, you really experience freedom and flight of soul, because without time there is also no structure, and that equals no stress.

So, something else to look for as you move into the 5th dimension is your desire for less structure, an unwillingness to commit to things in advance, more desire to live in and to enjoy the moment as you are in that moment, and appreciating everything that comes your way, knowing that it is part of your journey created by you. When you begin to experience this, you are absolutely going to love it!

I receive emails asking that I pray at a certain time on a certain day, to join in a world wide prayer thing. It's a wonderful thing, but it just never feels comfortable to me because I feel that I am in a constant state of prayer, a constant state of prayer with no structure.

I open the refrigerator and thank God for the refrigerator that keeps our food fresh. I thank God for a comfortable bed with clean sheets and a nice soft blanket to keep me warm, for a roof over our heads, for looking after our family and friends, and on and on, always asking God to bless our Planet Earth and all living things. And, so, being in a constant state of prayer, the idea of praying at a certain time on a certain day to me is stifling, it's structure and it's not comfortable for me. It takes away the feeling of freedom and flight of soul. Just thinking about it brings me down to the 3rd dimension, but thinking about Dr. Peebles and the rest takes me right back to the 5th. I'm not putting down group prayer at all. It's wonderful and totally effective, no doubt about it. However, where there is no time or space, all of our prayers, the frequency/energy of our prayers are all out there together all the time. I tell my clients when I work with them that the energy that I am working with during our healing session goes out into the Universe and they can draw on that healing energy whenever they want to. It works.

It's important to understand that time does not exist in the 5th dimension, nor does structure: only joy, freedom and flight of soul, light, light and more light.

You will get tired. After all, you are transitioning from the 3rd to the 5th dimension within self. You will need to allow your body to catch up with the changes occurring within you.

As you move into the 5th dimension you may notice that you are not analyzing yourself or others quite so much, because . . . you are having more and more loving allowance for yourself and others. (The first of the Three

Principles.) Somewhere along the way you finally realize that you really don't have to save the world, that your only job here is to step into your world by being all that you are, realizing the light, the love and the God that you are and again, sharing all that you are with the world. What the world and what God wants from you is you.

Chapter 7

THINGS TO LOOK FOR ALONG THE WAY

Your need to ask so many questions will diminish. Questions and answers are simply different sides of the same coin, because if you have the question you have the answer there inside of you. This is truth.

When I started out, I had so many questions, I wanted to know everything there is to know about spiritual healing. I took classes and read more books than you could count, on all kinds of healing modalities. Then one day I realized that whenever I had a question on anything at all, that question would run through my consciousness and lo and behold that question would be answered. Someone would make a comment, a situation would occur giving me the answer, or the answer would simply pop into my consciousness. This didn't happen overnight. It took a lot of quiet time on my part, a lot of meditation, and a whole lot of trust in myself before I actually believed and trusted when I heard the answers to my questions from my heart. And, if I didn't hear the answer right away, I knew that my question would be answered one way or another when it was time for me to have the answer. This also takes awareness. You never know where or how your answer will come to you, so be aware of everything around you

As you move into the 5th dimension your need for asking questions outside of yourself diminishes as you realize that you already have the answers inside you. And, now, because you are lightening up as you continue moving forward, and you are better able to go within, when a question comes into your consciousness, be still and listen, trust that you do have the answer and it will be given to you in whatever form necessary for you to understand. You will know this more and more as you become more and more a part of the 5th dimension, and it becomes easier and easier for you to go deep within and to trust you.

As your trust in yourself increases, your trust in all things naturally increases as well, as the honest echo of you is being reflected back to you. It's a win/win situation. Therefore your need to know "why" eventually leaves as you trust more and more in "what is." It is what it is, things are what they are, it doesn't matter why. The idea is to just relax and enjoy what is. There is no need or desire to ask God the why of things when you trust God and you know that things are exactly as they should be, as you are living in the now and enjoying every moment of that living.

As you work with the Three Principles and feel yourself moving into the 5th dimension, be aware of the changes going on within you. Be aware of the changes occurring in how you look at things, how you feel, how you handle situations, and how you regard others, family, friends. As your capacity for compassion for all things continues to expand, notice how your life is changing. Be aware of you, and you will know exactly where you are on your journey to the 5th dimension. And remember: it's a gradual journey.

Our spirit is so much larger than our physical body, and now, in our journey to the 5th dimension we are expanding our spirit, making it more and more a part of us. We are stepping not only into the 5th dimension, but we are stepping more and more into ourselves.

During your journey into the 5th Dimension you experience a larger part of yourself, of who you really are. You begin to walk in peace, in a knowing, a knowing that you ARE peace, you ARE love, you ARE compassion and that wherever you are healing, peace, love and compassion are there as well, and the healing of whatever is out of balance takes place within you, and for those around you. That's what happens as the things of the 3rd dimension dissipate, as you move closer and closer into the 5th dimension, a space of love, peace and compassion.

Things fall into place more easily because you are allowing it, you are not trying to control things, you are trusting God, and knowing deep within that everything is in right order; that things are exactly as they should be at any given moment, no matter how things look.

Moving into the 5th dimension is a gradual journey. All of the above have happened to me over a period of who knows how long, more years than I care to count. Now the movement is speeded up with our Planet Earth moving into the 5th dimension, and taking those who want to go along for the ride with her.

The finer points of energy are what you experience as you move along on this journey. Notice the change within yourself. The slowing down, the understanding of so many things you never understood before, the peace, the deep knowing within of things you just wondered about before on your journey back to God.

You realize more and more that your healing is really up to you, that the only healing that is lasting is the healing that you create for yourself from within, and that is exactly what is happening as you journey toward the 5th dimension.

Chapter 8
WHY DO I WANT TO DO THIS?

Oh my goodness! I don't even know where to begin.

First of all, you won't be aware of the process of the change within you, until suddenly one day you realize things are different.

Your world will be easier, happier, free of pain and dis-ease; you will experience freedom and flight of soul as never before. Because you are choosing to walk away from your 3rd dimensional thoughts and beliefs and move forward into the 5th, your priorities will become more and more clear to you. You will understand the importance of family and friends, you will understand that we are all here together as one, learning as we go, as you experience the joy of sharing all that you are with the world around you, as we draw upon and share our resources.

You will enjoy the simplicity of just living. You will revel in the absence of structure where time does not exist. For me, I think that is the greatest joy, the absence of structure. I am a nature girl at heart, and am blessed by living in a rural area alive with a great variety of birds, rabbits running around, a Javelina every now and then, not to mention a few coyotes. With the structure pretty much gone from my life, I spend a whole lot of time just watching nature. I put a large saucer of water out for the birds and cut up carrots for the rabbits. I never understood the "bird watchers" in my youth, but now . . . now I see the fascination. I never tire of watching them, all the different species, quail, doves, sparrows, a beautiful oriole just to name a few, interacting with one another, sometimes in a good way, sometimes in a bit of an ornery way, sometimes as many as eight or ten birds trying to take a bath all at the same time in that saucer of water I put out for them.

Another thing I've found really interesting in this living without structure thing (and I'm lovin' it) is if I don't feel like doing something, I don't do it. I wait until I do feel like doing it, and guess what? Everything always gets done when it needs to! It's totally amazing. No stress, no strain, no rush, no fuss, just a whole lot of fun. You're going to love this no-structure living.

There's more.

You will find joy in the little things, although at this point in your journey you may now consider them to be big things. You will find joy in the intricacy of a beautiful flower, the vivid colors of a bird, a beautiful sunset, or the sparkling smile of a little child. You'll choose to sit and watch the movement of the clouds through a beautiful blue sky, or listen to the rustling of the leaves of a tree. You will find joy in the simple things amid the chaos going on in the world around you in governments, financial institutions and all the rest.

In your meditations you will feel so full of love, as if you are right there with the Angels—a place filled with light and loaded with love, a place of finer and more refined energy, a lighter and more love-filled dimension. Yes, there you are, in the 5th dimension.

Long story short, you will be living in the now, not worrying about things that went on yesterday, or wondering what tomorrow may bring. You will have left all of that behind in the 3rd dimension. The 5th dimension is all about living in the now.

You can look forward to living your life in abundance as you are ridding yourself of the illusions of separation. This is the real abundance of abiding in the eternal. There are no borders, barriers or boundaries so you will experience freedom and flight of soul as never before. You will have glimpses of the 5th dimension, periods of time existing there as you expand your consciousness, and once you have experienced this (and you will), you will never forget it. Because our learning never ends, there will always be things for us to work through. But it will be easier and less painful as you remember the feeling of being in the 5th dimension; that memory giving you a whole lot of incentive to get back there. (Yes, we do jump from dimension to dimension all the time depending on where we choose to be in our consciousness.)

Because there is no time, and no structure, you can enjoy a stress free life as you live in the now. No thought of yesterday or tomorrow, just enjoying each moment as it presents itself. Can you even imagine the freedom of living this way?

Emotion fades as you are able to see things as they are, i.e., it is what it is; things just are what they are, and always in right order. Yes, emotion fades, but not caring, concern, love, or compassion. These things are founded on love, and just keep expanding within you. You'll live in the moment knowing that everything is exactly as it should be; there is no need for worry. That, too, diminishes as you grow into this knowing.

Time technology is going to change. In corporations the way in which time is perceived will change and structure will disappear. As things crumble and are rebuilt, we will be working out of our homes if we choose. Corporations will be run on an ebb and flow basis instead of the structure of the clock, allowing for employees to work according to their own physical natural rhythms, working the hours that best suit their ebb and flow of life. It's the freedom and the balance within the human form that will be considered and promoted within corporations. It's about 20 years down the line, however, before things are really going to shift.

There will still be things that need to be done, but they too will be done in the natural flow of life according to you.

You can look forward to an increase in telepathic communication and proof, scientific evidence of Spirit.

Your dreams will become more vivid.

You will be able to see into this finer and less dense environment.

You will be filled with love for the world.

You will be excited in anticipating what's coming up next for you.

You will be experiencing a life of fun and full of enthusiasm for all of it.

The 5th dimension is a journey into, and revealing more of, you to the world.

Chapter 9

ARE THERE 5TH DIMENSIONAL BEINGS HERE WITH US NOW?

Yes, absolutely. There are many walking among us who are already experiencing the 5th dimension in various degrees, a lot of them children. These people may not realize it, but you might. They are the ones existing here with us and incorporating God's love in every aspect of their lives. If you do some really deep introspection, you may find that you are one of them.

The children that I'm talking about here are the ones we know as the Indigo and Crystal children. These children are here with us now, learning to cope with living on Planet Earth, carrying within themselves the energies/ frequencies of the 5th dimension. A great many of these children (because our society does not understand them, and in many cases can't keep up with them) are diagnosed as ADD and other such things. There are droves of them coming in with special assignments in terms of what they are going to be teaching the world. We have already seen some of these children as genius artists, musicians and public speakers, all doing their thing at a very young age. Patience and time is what is needed now on our part while we wait for these children to grow up. They are the ones who are going to turn our system around. It will be about twenty years before the changes that these 5th dimensional beings are bringing to us will be in place. Right now they are looking at it, studying the flaws, seeing the problems that are created by separation within families, the destruction of certain social systems that worked beautifully for the earth at one time until they were taken advantage of, such as family, marriage, commitment, honor, integrity, responsibility, communication, love, gentleness, kindness, respect, and all things born of love. They are seeing that these things are lacking in the world. They have all of these things inside of them, but they're going to have to redesign everything in order to make the world a better place, and that will take time.

As they mature, they are going to have a hard time staying focused with time. They won't be teaching us as teachers per se, but by demonstration. It will be through our frustration with these children that we will learn patience and compassion and finally figure out just why these children function the way they do. It's not because the children are ADD or any such thing. It is because they are functioning very well without time and space, and they're trying very hard to fit themselves into a societal expectation that is not really working for anyone anymore. What we are experiencing here is the breaking down of a structure, and the building of a new one.

ADD? I don't think so. If you know any of these children and would like to help them, encourage them in their understandings. Tell them how wonderful they are, that you understand them and their difficulties here. They have come into a very 3rd dimensional world where so many children are being severely neglected, not given love, not given anything other than maybe some candy and some money and a few things to play with; not given the things that children require. They need love and attention; they need to know that they count. They have incarnated into this 3rd dimensional world with the characteristics of a 5th dimensional being. How horrendously difficult must that be? They're going to need a lot of help, a lot of patience and understanding, and as much love as we can possibly give. That's how they will be teaching.

Chapter 10

BE AWARE AND PAY ATTENTION

"It unfolds as you're writing" . . . that's the message I received in the beginning of this adventure. Well, let me tell you, that is pure unadulterated truth!

I finally stopped and pulled in the reins. I realized that I had fallen into a panic mode in trying to get this book finished, to get it out to those that may be helped by it as we journey into the 5th dimension.

All of the things I'd been writing about here came into play. How subtly we can be lured out of our relax, release and surrender mode. There I was enjoying my freedom and flight of soul to the hilt and "BAM!" instead of being in my heart and writing from there where the information flows smooth as honey, I'm back in my head and nothing is happening, no ideas, no insights, nothing! I spent about two days there in that space and then . . . I'm lying in bed and I hear . . . "Wait a minute, what's going on here? I'm not relaxed, I certainly am not releasing anything, and way not surrendering to God." No wonder nothing is happening, I'm back in my head instead of in my heart. The words aren't flowing, the insights aren't coming. In short . . . I'm a mess! I have created my very own "writer's block!"

Well, recognizing the problem, which I've heard is ninety percent of the solution, I hopped right back into the relax, release and surrender mode.

So, now I'm back, I am relaxed, I am releasing the expectations of having to have this book done within a certain time period, and I've totally surrendered everything to God and Spirit. In re-centering myself I know that I'm back in the flow, words and insights will come, and this book will be published at absolutely the right time, and be in the hands of whoever is looking for help in their transition into the 5th dimension.

This is a beautiful example of what happens when you lose sight of the real reality and get caught up in 3rd dimension expectations.

I was able to experience going from the edge of the 5th, back to the 3rd and then back to the 5th. I experienced going from joy to pain, light to heavy, clarity to confusion. I went from everything working to nothing working; I was totally out of the flow while in the 3rd dimension. I was given the opportunity to feel, really feel, the difference of residing in the 5th dimension as compared to the 3rd. I felt it physically, mentally, emotionally and spiritually.

The 5th dimension is a state of absolute joy, and does it ever feel good to be back, relaxed, releasing and surrendering!

In the beginning, Dr. Peebles asked that I set aside my life in favor of writing this book, and I was more than happy to do what he asked, and in the end I found that I had not set my life aside at all, but instead have been growing more fully into it as I write.

Whatever it takes for you to journey to the 5th dimension is so worth it. Once you start experiencing it, you will agree, and never even consider looking back! It's all that I have talked about and shared with you, and to quote my teacher and guide for the past ten years, Dr. James Martin Peebles, "My dears, this is just the tip of the iceberg."

Epilogue

So, what we are doing here is changing our minds, deciding to leave the heavy negative mish mash of the 3rd dimension, and move forward toward and into the 5th. We do create our own reality with our thoughts, deeds and words. What are your thoughts, words and deeds based in? What energy band are you traveling in at any given moment? Every time our mood changes we have stepped into a different band of energy, be it anger, joy, resentment, hate, love, compassion. Each is its own band of energy, and you step in and out of them by your choices and perceptions.

Change your mind, and change your life. You can stay in the 3rd dimension with its anger, jealousies, judgments, greed and all the rest, or, you can change your mind and step into the energy band of love, joy, compassion, self love, happiness and all the rest there, and enjoy freedom and flight of soul. And, you can't even imagine that feeling until you've experienced it.

The thing is, as you choose the bands of life without pain, you find that the 3rd dimensional energies simply fall away, they disintegrate and are replaced almost without notice on your part with the bands of love. One day something will happen. I don't know what, I don't remember how it happened to me, but one day all of a sudden I realized so many of the third dimensional habits were gone. They had just simply disappeared almost without notice, and the feeling of real freedom and flight of soul was overwhelming. There is no way I can share that feeling here with just words.

This is a very exciting time for us, a time of increased scientific discovery activated by conditions on earth, and a need to grow bringing about more and more validation of Spirit with scientific proof and evidence.

Throughout your journey, keep in mind that there is no hierarchy in any of this. There is never hierarchy in any of it: one place, one spirit, one teacher, all the same, all of the same importance in our journey of dissolving the illusion of separation—and, there is always more.

Well, that's about it. I have been given the opportunity to experience the 3rd and the 5th dimensions back to back, to feel the difference, the heaviness, the uneasiness of being in the 3rd, and the lightness and joy of being in the 5th. Once you experience the 5th dimension you will so want to stay there, you will do everything in your power to keep moving forward in order for you to experience it as much as possible.

We are all on this wild ride together, learning and teaching all at the same time. Learning from our family, our friends, our relationships, learning from everything around us. It is indeed a wild ride, and a fun ride, when you realize that what's happening in your life is what needs to happen in order for you to learn what you came here to Planet Earth to learn.

Pay attention to everything. I am the same as any of you reading this book, I am simply a human being having a spiritual experience here in this human body. Yes, I'm different than a lot of you, because I am married for 57 years now with three grown children, nine grandchildren, five great-grandchildren, siblings and an interesting variety of friends. However, I am still a human being, as you are a human being, inviting into my life those experiences that have taken me into the 5th dimension of freedom and out of the box of the 3rd dimension. Every experience I have had has been a learning one. I have learned from every person in my life, all my dreams and plans taking form as my life is enhanced by every one of my life experiences. Look at your experiences, examine what you have learned so far, embrace Dr. Peebles' Three Principles and take that wild ride into the 5th dimension. And, when you have experienced the magic, continue on your journey here on Planet Earth as I am doing, living your life, experiencing the finer points of energy that is the 5th dimension, as you teach and show the world the new you.

It's your choice.

"Example is not the main thing in influencing others. It is the only thing."
—Albert Schweitzer

I hope you enjoyed our trip to the 5th dimension, that you have learned something along the way. And, I look forward to seeing you there.

With much love and joy,

Beverly Scott

Addendem

WHAT ARE DIMENSIONS AND HOW DO THEY FIGURE IN OUR LIVES?

We've pretty much covered the 3rd and the 5th dimensions, but what about the rest? How do dimensions in general figure in our lives? How many are there, what are they, where are they? Up to this point I've shared what I know about the 3rd and the 5th dimensions, and our journey from here to there. Now I would like to expand on the subject of dimensions just a little bit more.

There are more dimensions than anyone could ever imagine. For instance, each individual carries a dimension of their own. When you were born you created a resonance in the world. Think of the wave created by a stone thrown into the water, and you see the radiation of that stone, the resonance of it propelling out into the Universe forever. It doesn't stop when the ripples on the water stop. You have just created another dimension. Your children are born, and they each create new dimensions. New dimensions are being created all the time. Now, to better understand what I'm talking about here, think of dimensions in terms of pictures that are made up of pixels, and inside of each pixel there is another picture, and inside of that picture are pixels, inside of those pixels there is another picture, it goes on like that without end. So do dimensions. This is really the best illustration I can think of to give you an understanding of how dimensions work. As you are picturing this in your mind, add the thought that you (as part of the Universe and its dimensions) are one of those pictures/pixels, and if one of those pictures/pixels is taken away, is missing, it would throw everything out of balance. That's how important you are in the scheme of things here in the oneness of the Universe residing here on Planet Earth in the 3rd dimension.

And, how does this all fit into our process of expansion on our journey back to God, discovering and dissolving the illusion of separation, discovering the god that we are? This is how we grow, this is how we learn about and experience the different parts of us. We are eternal beings, we are light beings, the part of us that we are experiencing here in the 3rd dimension on Planet Earth is just a fraction, a very small fraction of who and what we really are. We visit whatever dimension we choose, depending on what part of our selves we want to experience. We do not necessarily go from dimension to dimension linearly; we can skip around if we choose. As you arrive into a new dimension where you have decided to go to grow and expand yourself imagine the unfolding of a flower. First you are folded into yourself, the light that you are, you experience what you have chosen to experience as you expand yourself and you blossom into bloom. You stand there in the light of God, then the flower dies, but your spirit continues, is absorbed back into the light and into yet another dimension, one that you have chosen to experience, to learn from, and to continue your expansion into the Oneness. And so it goes as we make our way from dimension to dimension, folding into ourselves, blossoming into bloom, the flower dying as the experience is complete, and our spirit being absorbed back into the light once more, and chooses to reincarnate into yet another dimension for an experience of our choosing.

If you can imagine the Oneness made up of millions and millions of dimensions, and we are that Oneness, and so each dimension is a part of us, and we are a part of each dimension, you can start to get the picture of how many parts of us there are for us to explore, just a little bit mind boggling to say the least. We do have a lot of help through this whole process however. If there are times that we don't know what area of our self we would like to experience or explore, while we are in what I call the "time out or resting period" dimension, there are many, many spirits and guides, teachers and Masters around to help us. It would be like they all gather around to share what they know of the different dimensions, and while they are sharing you hear something that catches your interest and bingo, you decide you want to go and experience that particular part of you, that particular part of yourself. So a group of spirits, guides, light body friends all get together with you and work out the best way for you to experience what you have chosen to experience and help you on your way. You are never alone in any part of your journey, you always have your Angels and guides with you, watching over you, and ready to help you. They will not do the work for you but they are ready to help and guide you through it.

It isn't necessary to go through all of the dimensions, and you can go through them at your own pace, some more rapidly than others depending on your understanding. It's like any other school: if you're on the fast track, and really get what's going on, you may even skip a dimension or two.

It is impossible for me to even try to get a handle on the Universe, the dimensions, or how it all works, but what I do know is that incorporating Dr. Peebles' Three Principles in tandem in your daily life, and staying in the moment, works. All you need is right there: Loving allowance for all things to be in their own time and place starting for yourself; increase communication with all of life, with respect; and self responsibility for your life as a creative adventure, for through your choices and perceptions you do, indeed, create your own reality.

Yes, it's all there, simple, but not easy. Not easy, because we humans are so resistant.

So try it, relax, release and surrender, trust and enjoy the journey, we have a long way to go.

FOR YOUR CONSIDERATION

If you are not familiar with meditation or have a problem getting out of your head and into your heart, toning will help you. If you are not familiar with toning and would like to learn more about it, then please visit my website at *http://simplespirituality.net* where you can read about "The Limitless Power of Toning".

I have also written a booklet and created a CD as a set. The booklet explains what toning is and how to begin your toning adventure, the CD contains a guided meditation to guide you into a meditative state, and on into toning with me as I tone.

Toning is a very quick and easy way to go deep within, to relax, release and surrender to all that is. It will help you to drop from your head down into your heart easier than anything I know, and will add a whole new dimension to your journey to the 5th.

Printed in Great Britain
by Amazon

57819770R00041